Zoom into Science

by Kathy Furgang

 HOUGHTON MIFFLIN HARCOURT

PHOTOGRAPHY CREDITS: COVER ©Todd Bannor/Alamy Images; 3 (b) ©Lana Sundman/Alamy Images; 4 (bl) ©Fstop/Alamy Images; 5 (t) ©Fstop/Alamy Images; 6 (b) ©saxpix.com/age fotostock; 7 (t) ©Todd Bannor/Alamy Images; 8 (t) ©Fstop/Alamy Images; 9 (t) ©Andres Rodriguez/Alamy Images; 10 (b) ©H. Mark Weidman Photography/Alamy Images; 11 (t) ©Don Despain/Alamy Images; 12 (t) ©Lana Sundman/Alamy Images; 13 (b) ©Ian Miles/Alamy Images

Printed in U.S.A.

ISBN: 978-0-544-07290-9

3 4 5 6 7 8 9 10 1083 21 20 19 18 17 16 15 14

4500470116   A B C D E F

Contents

Vocabulary

experiment   empirical evidence

hypothesis

model

variable

data

Stretch Vocabulary

trials

verify

Introduction

Have you ever wondered what kinds of jobs scientists have? They work all around the world in different places. Some scientists work in laboratories. No matter where they work, all scientists ask questions about the world. Then scientists make a plan to find out the answer to their questions.

Think about the scientists who work in laboratories that make sure cars are safe to drive. These scientists also test to see whether the cars work as they should. Like all scientists, they experiment to find the answers to their questions. They follow special steps to do their experiments.

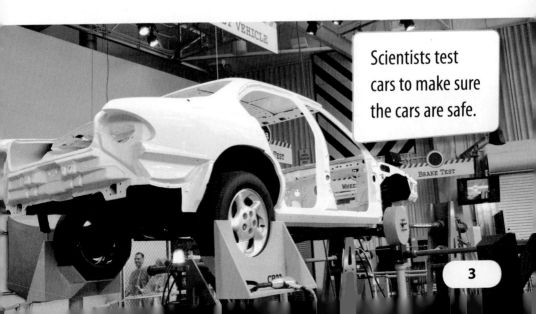

Scientists test cars to make sure the cars are safe.

Go Ahead and Ask It!

What's so important about asking questions? It gets people thinking. Scientists at a car-testing laboratory think about car safety. That's very important. The scientists ask questions about what might make a car safer. Then they think about how they can answer those questions.

Every few years, car companies build new types of cars. The companies hope to make each type better than the last. Scientists may test many things related to the safety of the car. For example, they may test how long the car takes to stop when it is moving at different speeds. They observe how all cars stop and start. They compare the brakes on the new car to the brakes on the older car. Then they ask an important question: "Will this new car stop faster or slower than the old car?" The scientists will investigate to find out.

Some scientists work together, while others work alone. But all scientists follow the same general steps to answer their questions.

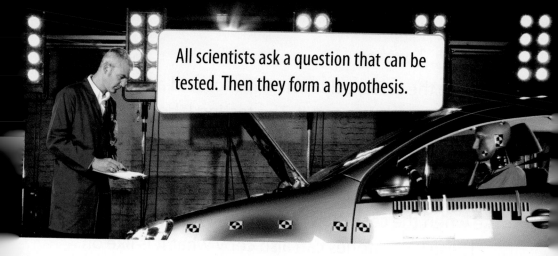

All scientists ask a question that can be tested. Then they form a hypothesis.

Word of the Day: Hypothesis

A hypothesis is a scientist's possible answer to a question. A hypothesis must be capable of being tested. To form a hypothesis, the scientists use what they know about how a car stops. Car-safety scientists gather and compare data about the new version of the car. They examine and test the brakes of the new car to figure out whether its brakes work better than the brakes of the old car.

Scientists use this information to form a hypothesis. A hypothesis is a statement. Their hypothesis is, "The brakes on the new version of the car will stop the car more quickly than those on the older one." The scientists do not yet know whether their hypothesis is supported. They will find out when they experiment.

Testing, Testing

Once the safety scientists have formed a hypothesis, they make a plan to test it. The testing laboratory is a model of what it is like on real roads. Instead of long roadways like the ones outdoors, the laboratories have rolling roadways. Large fans are used to show what it is like when the car drives on windy days.

These laboratories can also copy what it is like on different types of roads: a smooth road, a bumpy road, or even a hill. Scientists use models to control the results of their tests. Using a laboratory also makes it easier to measure such things as how long it takes the cars to stop. It could be difficult and unsafe to do some car testing on real roads.

Laboratories are safe places for scientists to test cars.

TRACTION

The scientists must carefully control everything about the investigation.

When scientists investigate, they think about the variable they are testing. The variable is the one thing that changes in the experiment. In this test of braking time, the type of brakes is the variable. Everything else in the experiment must stay the same. The scientists decide to find out how quickly each type of brakes can stop a car moving at 100 kilometers per hour (62 miles per hour). Each car must have the same kind of tires. Each car must hold the same amount of weight inside it. The conditions of the road must also stay the same for each car. Both cars will stop on the same flat, smooth roadway. The only thing that changes each time is the brakes of the car being tested.

The crash-test dummies are used to investigate how real cars work.

Investigation Time

The scientists set up a test. It's almost like testing the cars on a real road. However, it's not always safe to use people in investigations. Instead, the scientists use models of people, called "crash-test dummies." By using these models, the scientists can study the effects of the new brakes without putting actual people in danger.

The scientists measure exactly how long it takes for each car to stop. They do ten trials, or tests, for each car. If the plan is followed the same way each time, the trials should have very similar results. Repeating the testing helps scientists make sure their conclusions are accurate.

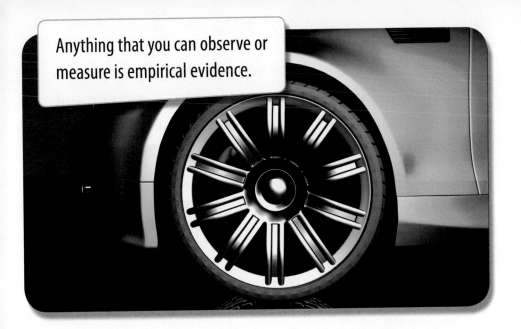

Anything that you can observe or measure is empirical evidence.

With each trial of the investigation, the scientists record their data. Data are pieces of information that scientists gather as they work. The measurements are the empirical evidence in their study. Empirical evidence is something that can be observed or measured. It is information that helps the scientists draw conclusions about their investigation. The scientists compare the empirical evidence to conclude how the brakes are different from each other.

And the Conclusion Is ...

When scientists look at their results, they may see a pattern, or a result that is repeated. In this experiment, scientists found that the brakes on the new car stopped the car faster than the brakes on the old car did. The scientists studied the data. The brakes on the new car are about three seconds faster than the ones on the old car. These results support the scientists' hypothesis.

Not all investigations support the hypothesis that is being tested. Scientists must look at their data to understand why they got the results they did. The scientists may want to change their test if they think they did something wrong during their testing. Or they may conclude that the first hypothesis was wrong and propose another solution to the same problem.

The scientists study data from the investigation to help them draw a conclusion.

After testing, scientists' conclusions point the way to safer cars and trucks.

Scientists must think about their data carefully. What can they conclude about their results? Could they conclude that all new cars stop faster than the older ones? No. The scientists can draw a conclusion only about the study they did. They conclude that the brakes on the new car were built better than the brakes on the older car. They have data to back up their conclusion. They did not just guess that the new brakes were better. They tested their hypothesis with a scientific investigation.

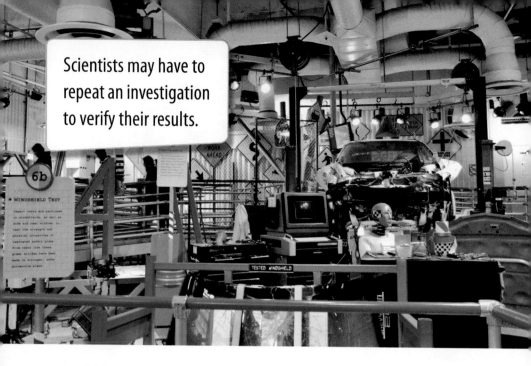

Scientists may have to repeat an investigation to verify their results.

Do That Again!

Scientists do not stop when they are finished with an investigation. Often, they may repeat the whole investigation to make sure that they get the same results again. In this way, scientists verify, or make sure, that the results were correct. The scientists may not get exactly the same measurements during each trial. However, if their conclusion was accurate, their results should be very similar. The scientists should come to the same conclusion the second time they do the investigation.

Don't Forget to Share

Once the investigation's results are verified, scientists share what they have found. They may use charts and bar graphs to display results. Other scientists may be able to use the data to help in their own investigations. Sharing results also helps scientists think of new questions to ask. Scientists may want to repeat the test when the car is going up a hill. They may repeat the test when the car is on bumpy ground or in the wind or rain. Their results may give carmakers ideas about how to make cars safer.

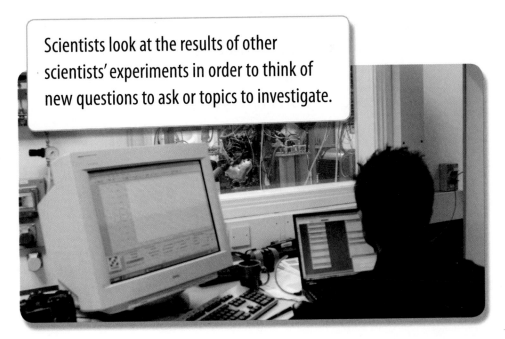

Scientists look at the results of other scientists' experiments in order to think of new questions to ask or topics to investigate.

Investigate a Question

Ask a question about something in your natural world. Choose something in nature or something you have seen move or change. Then form a hypothesis to answer the question. With your teacher's help, plan an investigation that can test your idea. Use the same steps the scientists in the book followed.

Write Your Results

Write the results of your investigation. Were you able to make a plan and test it? Did your results support your hypothesis? Why or why not? Write any new questions that you thought of during your investigation.

Glossary

data [DAY•tuh] Individual facts, statistics, and items of information.

empirical evidence [em•PEER•i•kul EV•uh•duhns] Data that is collected during an investigation and that can be observed or measured.

experiment [ek•SPAIR•uh•muhnt] A test done to see whether a hypothesis is correct.

hypothesis [hy•PAHTH•uh•sis] A possible answer to a question that can be tested to see if it is correct.

model [MAH•dul] A representation of something real that is too big or too small or that has too many parts to be studied directly.

observe [uhb•ZERV] To use your senses to gather information.

trial [TRY•uhl] A test to see how well something performs.

variable [VAIR•ee•uh•bul] The one thing that changes in an experiment.

verify [VAIR•uh•fy] To make sure that something is true or accurate.